AF796738

Finding and Forming Sponsors and Godparents

Finding and Forming Sponsors and Godparents

Edited by
James A. Wilde

Liturgy Training Publications

Copyright ©1988 Archdiocese of Chicago. All rights reserved.
Liturgy Training Publications, 1800 North Hermitage Avenue,
Chicago IL 60622-1101

Printed in the United States of America
ISBN 0-930467-77-9

Art: *Carol Joslin*
Book design: *Jane Caplan*

Contents

Introduction | 1

James A. Wilde

Canonical Qualifications
of Sponsors and Godparents | 5

John M. Huels

Sponsors
Begetting Sponsors | 13

Sandra A. Chakeres

Finding Sponsors
and Godparents | 17

James A. Wilde

Liturgical Formation
of Sponsors and Godparents | 23

Julia Upton

Adult Conversion
and the Ministry of Sponsor | 29

Edward Sellner

Spiritual Formation
of Sponsors and Godparents | 41

James A. Wilde

Forming Sponsors
and Godparents in the Ministry
of Peace and Justice | 47
Mary Evelyn Jegen

Hispanic Traditions
of *Padrinos* and *Madrinas* | 57
Arturo J. Perez

Bibliography | 63

Contributors | 69

Introduction

Sponsors and godparents are nothing new in the church. They aren't the invention of the charismatic movement, Vatican II or the Rite of Christian Initiation of Adults, (RCIA). In fact, according to the Acts of the Apostles, sponsors and godparents go back to about six years after the death and resurrection of Christ.

Barnabas

> When Saul arrived in Jerusalem he tried to join the disciples, but they were afraid of him and did not believe he was a disciple. Then Barnabas took charge of him and escorted him to the apostles, and he reported to them how on the way Saul had seen the Lord and spoken to him, and how in Damascus he had spoken out boldly in the name of Jesus.
>
> — *Acts 9:26–27*

Some months later, news of Saul's great success adding numbers to the church of Antioch reached the church of Jerusalem, and they sent Barnabas to check on the matter. Barnabas found Saul in Tarsus, brought him back to Antioch where for a whole year they both met with the church there and successfully reached another large number of people. It was at Antioch that disciples were first called Christians (see Acts 11:19–26).

With Saul, Barnabas carried the collection back to Jerusalem for the poor (Acts 11:29–30). Saul and Barnabas were selected with others to proclaim the good news in cities the news had not yet reached (Acts 13:1–14:28). At Lystra they were acclaimed as gods—Barnabas as Zeus, Paul as Hermes—and then they were thrown out of the city by stoning (Acts 14:8–20). Both Barnabas and Paul were selected as official representatives at the Council of Jerusalem around the year 50 (Acts 15:1–35).

According to Paul himself, it was Barnabas and Peter who at first refused to eat with the Gentiles (Galatians 2:13–14). The separation of Paul and Barnabas took place over the question of traveling companions. A sharp disagreement arose; Barnabas went to Cyprus with John Mark, and Paul went his way with Silas (Acts 15:36–41). From

Philemon 24, 1 Corinthians 9:6 and 2 Timothy 4:11, however, we can conclude that the disagreement between Paul and Barnabas was finally healed.

Barnabas is our clearest example of a sponsor and godparent. Barnabas bore witness to Paul's worthiness among the disciples in Jerusalem. He introduced Paul to the apostles. He was a companion to Paul, walking with him through honor and disgrace in a ministry of love for all people.

Hippolytus of Rome

The second part of *The Apostolic Tradition* by Hippolytus of Rome who died in about the year 237 is very revealing. The words *sponsor* or *godparent* are still not used. Instead, the term *those who introduce the inquirer* is used throughout. And the primary function of those who introduce the inquirer is to give testimony about the inquirer's former state of life. Whole classes of people—such as pimps, teachers of pagan philosophy, pagan priests, most soldiers, makers of idols or amulets, sculptors, painters and men with concubines—may not be accepted into the order of learners (catechumens) unless they forsake their styles of life. Those who introduce the inquirer are fully responsible. The bishop, presbyter or deacon are not mentioned in this connection.

Evidently the church preferred to remain small in numbers rather than diminish in quality. Its severity regarding catechumens seems to honor the church, the word and the eucharist—not to reflect hostility to sinners. Only their sin was the issue. And it was this major issue over which *those who introduce them* and the catechists had authority.

The success of the three-year catechumenate of *The Apostolic Tradition* was measured primarily by the *conduct* of the catechumen, and it was those who brought them—along with the catechists—who made the final judgment. As the inquirer's life is examined, those who brought them testify whether "they respected widows, visited the sick, practiced all the good works. If those who introduced the candidates testify that they have been living in this way, let them hear the gospel." Two further responsibilities of those who introduced the candidates is that they help dry and clothe the neophyte at baptism and that they continue to give testimony about the person's conduct for a number of years after initiation. The point is clear: for Hippolytus of Rome, saint and martyr, giving testimony about conduct over a span of several years is the main task of those who introduce inquirers (Michel Dujarier, "Sponsorship," in *Adult Baptism and the Catechumenate*, ed. Johannes Wagner, Concilium 22, pp. 45–50).

For the most part, the *Gelasian Sacramentary*, 316, and *Ordo Romanus XI* (Andrieu's edition) in their eighth century final form tell us that the church of Rome still followed Hippolytus' pattern of initiation (see Aidan Kavanagh, *The Shape of Baptism: The Rite of Christian Initiation*, pp. 54, 74).

Children

Also in the fourth century, the practice of baptizing children of parents who were baptized became popular. The wave of such family initiations made sponsors for infants and children very important. Their function, as opposed to sponsors of adults, was to oversee the spiritual welfare of the infant or child in case of negligence or incapacity of the parents.

Variations

Over 20 centuries the responsibilities and functions of sponsors varied and sometimes waned close to nothing. Since Vatican II the apostolic and spiritual companion aspect seems to be taking prominence. With catechumens, sponsors are rediscovering the power of full participation in the liturgy in addition to the discussion of lectionary passages in groups. Through catechumens, sponsors are discovering some of the values of private prayer also. The wonder of simply praying to God in one's own words, the calm of centering prayer, the power and peace of the way of the breath, the contemplative prayer that is accessible to everyone—all these ways are so old and yet so new to some.

Work done for peace and justice, the ministry for those beyond my immediate reach, seemed almost unknown 25 years ago. Today, however, Christians know addresses of senators, Catholics work in soup kitchens and initiates know that as long as there are poor, there is a job to do: the preferential option for the poor. In basic ways, catechumens become the teachers of the sponsors and godparents.

If I learn from the model of Alcoholics Anonymous, my sacramental sponsorship calls for a personal dedication of companionship and friendship through rough times and smooth. It means sharing personal strengths in a most loving way. If I look closer at Barnabas, I learn that ultimate forgiveness is the key relationship between godparent and neophyte. If I look at Hippolytus, my main interest is observing how my catechumen acts so that I might bear proper witness.

♦ *James A. Wilde*

Canonical Qualifications of Sponsors and Godparents

An important office in the sacramental initiation of both adults and children is that of godparents. This essay considers the role and qualifications of godparents in light of the revised Code of Canon Law and the liturgical books. Initially it will be necessary to clarify exactly what is meant by the canonical godparent.

Sometimes the Latin word *patrinus* is rendered "sponsor" in English. However, the translation "godparent" is preferable because it clearly distinguishes this role from another one during the catechumenate, which is called in Latin the *sponsor.* This ministry, which is best translated "sponsor" in English, need not be fulfilled by the same person as the canonical *patrinus.* The presence of a sponsor for each candidate is required at the Rite of Acceptance into the Order of Catechumens. Often this sponsor is later chosen by the catechumen to be his or her godparent for the Rite of Election and for sacramental initiation, but it sometimes happens that the two persons are different as, for example, when the one who is going to be the official godparent is unable to attend the Rite of Acceptance into the Order of Catechumens.

Canonically the qualifications of the sponsor for the Rite of Acceptance into the Order of Catechumens are not strict. The sponsor must know the candidate, help him or her and witness to the candidate's morals, faith and intention (Rite of Christian Initiation of Adults, 10). The sponsor need not fulfill the other qualifications of the canonical godparent.

Role of Godparents

The role of godparents is treated in both the Code of Canon Law and the Roman Ritual. Their duties, which are distinct in infant and adult initiation, can be considered in three phases: the period of preparation or catechumenate, the celebration of the liturgy of initiation and the postbaptismal relationship.

The principal duty of godparents before *infant baptism* is to be properly instructed in the meaning of the sacrament and the obligations that are attached to it (canon 851, 1°). Ideally, the godparents should attend the prebaptismal instructions along with the parents, but if this is not possible, the minister can provide the necessary catechesis in the course of the homily during the celebration of baptism itself or make other arrangements to ensure that the godparents understand their role.

During the celebration of infant baptism, the chief duty of the godparent is simply to be present and profess the faith of the church. By their presence the godparents are "to represent both the expanded spiritual family of the one to be baptized and the role of the church as a mother" (General Introduction to Christian Initiation [GICI], 8). Together with the parents, they also profess the church's faith in which the child is being baptized (GICI, 9). When the godparents take an active part in the responses, prayers and song of the liturgy, their role as witnesses of the faith is more clearly evident.

The lifelong role of godparents is specified more by family or local custom than it is by canon law. The code states only that the godparent "will help the baptized to lead a Christian life in harmony with baptism and to fulfill faithfully the obligations connected with it" (canon 872). The Ritual adds that the godparent will be ready to help the parents so that children will come to profess the faith and live up to it (GICI, 8). Traditionally, the godparent has been understood as a person who would see to the Christian upbringing of the godchild in case the parent could no longer fulfill this responsibility.

At *adult initiation* the godparent plays a major role, beginning in the catechumenate. He or she is to be close to the catechumen, a friend, one whose example and character is a model of Christian life for the catechumen (RCIA, 11). It is desirable that the canonical godparents also be the sponsors during the rite of admission to the catechumenate if this is possible. In this rite the sponsors acknowledge their readiness to help the catechumens come to know and follow Christ, and they testify that the catechumens have chosen Christ as Lord and wish to serve him.

The public office of godparent begins at the Rite of Election when the church hears the godparents' testimony concerning the suitability of the catechumens. They testify to the Christian community that the catechumens have faithfully listened to the word of God, have been true to that word, have begun to walk in God's presence, have sought the fellowship of their brothers and sisters, have joined them in prayer and are worthy of admission to the sacraments of initiation. They are exhorted by the presider to continue helping the catechumens by their loving care and example. Throughout the catechumenate the godparents are to "show the candidates how to practice the gospel in personal and social life and to sustain them in moments of hesitancy and anxiety" (RCIA, 11).

During the celebration of the sacraments of initiation the godparents take an active role comparable to that of the parents at infant baptism. The godparent informs the presider of the name of the candidate, touches the candidate during or immediately after the immersion or infusion of water and presents the newly baptized with a candle lighted from the Easter candle.

In the Eastertime period of mystagogia, the godparents continue to play an important role by helping the neophytes to become included into the life of the community and by accompanying them to Sunday Mass. There is also an ongoing responsibility of the godparents to assist the neophytes to remain faithful to their baptismal promises. Ideally the special spiritual relationship between godparent and neophyte will last throughout their lives.

Qualifications

1. *Number and sex.* Ordinarily there should be one godparent for each person to be baptized, male or female, or there can be two godparents, one godmother and one godfather (canon 873). This excludes two godparents of the same sex or more than two godparents. (In countries where there are several godparents, only two should be recorded unless legitimate custom permits the recording of all the names.) In a case of necessity when no one is available to assume the role of godparent, anyone with the proper intention can baptize, but he or she should try to have at least one witness present who could testify to the fact that the baptism was validly conferred (canon 875). The proper intention is simply to do what the church does when it baptizes. Anyone with the use of reason can function as a witness.

   In some places it is customary to have two godparents at infant baptism and only one godparent for adult initiation, but there is nothing to prevent having two godparents for an adult or only one for an infant. The adult candidates themselves or the infant's parents or guardians should be free to determine whether they want one godparent or two.

2. *Designation and approval.* Godparents must have the intention of performing their role; that is, they must intend to assume an ongoing spiritual relationship with the baptized person and not merely function as a passive witness to the sacrament. In adult initiation, the godparents are chosen by the person to be baptized, and they must be approved by the local priest with, insofar as possible, the acceptance of the Christian community (canon 874,

§1, 1°; RCIA, 123, 11). Given the importance of the godparents in the process of adult initiation, it is imperative that only faithful Catholics who are fitting models of the Christian life be approved for this role.

For infant baptism, such a rigorous standard for approval of godparents is unnecessary because the parents are the primary models of faith for their children. The parents or guardians choose the godparents for infant baptism; in their absence, the pastor or minister of baptism can designate a qualified and willing person for this office. Although not required in canon law, the "sponsor certificate" signed by the godparent's pastor or his delegate is a common method for approving godparents. The sponsor certificate attests that a person is a member of the parish, is a practicing Catholic and is qualified to be a godparent.

3. *Age.* Godparents must be *at least sixteen,* unless the diocesan bishop has established another age or unless in an exceptional case it seems to the pastor or minister that there is just cause to admit a younger person (canon 874, §1, 2°). An example of just cause for admitting a younger person would be a close personal or family relationship. In such cases, those who are fourteen or fifteen could be godparents provided they fulfill all the other legal qualifications.

   In reference to baptism, those *fourteen and older* have a special place in canon law. The rites for "Christian Initiation of Children Who Have Reached Catechetical Age" (RCIA, 252–330) are to be followed for all who have the use of reason, which legally is presumed to be attained around the age of seven. However, those who are fourteen and older can choose their own rite of baptism, either the Latin rite or an Eastern rite Catholic church (canon 111, §2), and they are to be referred to the bishop so that he may celebrate their sacramental initiation if he judges it expedient (canon 863). Fourteen was the standard minimal age to be a godparent in the law of the 1917 code. It is also the age at which a woman can marry validly in the church. (Men must be sixteen.) Because the age of fourteen indicates in the law the attainment of a certain degree of maturity, and because the role of godparent is that of a mature Christian, it does not seem advisable, even with good reason, to approve a godparent who is younger than fourteen.

4. *Fully initiated Catholic.* Godparents must be Catholic, whether of the Latin rite or an Eastern rite, and they must have received the sacraments of confirmation and eucharist (canon 874, §1, 3°). A Catholic is anyone who has been baptized into the Catholic church or who has been received into full communion with it.

   The *Ecumenical Directory,* 48, provides one exception to this rule, namely, for separated Eastern Christians, commonly called the Orthodox. A suitable Eastern Orthodox can be a godparent at the baptism of a Catholic, provided there is also a Catholic godparent designated, and as long as the Catholic upbringing of the one to be baptized is assured. Reciprocally a Catholic can be a godparent at a baptism in a separated Eastern Orthodox church along with an Eastern Orthodox godparent. In either case, the responsibility for seeing to the Christian upbringing of the baptized person belongs primarily to the godparent who belongs to the church in which the person was baptized.

   Protestants may not be godparents at the baptism of a Catholic, but a validly baptized Protestant can be admitted and recorded as a *witness* together with the Catholic godparent (canon 874, §2). Protestants are treated differently in canon law than Eastern Orthodox Christians because the latter are considered to be more closely in communion with the Catholic church than Protestants are.

5. *In good standing.* Godparents must lead a life of faith in harmony with the undertaking of their role (canon 874, §1, 3°). As noted above, a higher standard should be required of godparents for adult initiation than for infant baptism. Explicitly excluded from being a godparent is anyone who has incurred a canonical penalty that has been lawfully imposed or declared by competent ecclesiastical authority (canon 874, §1, 4°).

   Very often it is difficult in large parishes for the priest issuing a sponsor certificate to know who truly is living a life of faith in harmony with this role. The best way to assure that this requirement is met is to impress upon the parents or adult catechumens the necessity of choosing a proper model as godparent, and the parish priest will then be in a better position to trust their judgment and not doubt the suitability of the person chosen.

Can divorced and remarried persons be godparents, or is their status incompatible with this role? Formerly, divorced and remarried persons in the United States incurred the penalty of excommunication, but this penalty was lifted in 1977. However, a divorced and remarried person who does not have an annulment or dissolution is living in an irregular second union that is said to contradict objectively the teachings of Christ and the church. Nevertheless, many divorced and remarried persons are very faithful and active Catholics. Some are in the process of seeking an annulment or dissolution of their previous marriage. Some have even been pastorally assisted to return in good conscience to full sacramental participation in the life of the church by means of the internal forum solution. Thus one cannot say unconditionally that all divorced and remarried persons are unworthy of being godparents. Like other Catholics, their suitability must be judged on a case by case basis.

6. *Not a parent*. A godparent may not be the father or mother of the person being baptized. The role of the parents and godparents are distinct. Christian parents have the primary responsibility for the Christian upbringing of their children; the godparents serve in an auxiliary role except at adult initiation where frequently the parents are not themselves Catholics. There is nothing in the 1983 code to prevent spouses, clergy or religious from being godparents.

Confirmation

The qualifications for godparents at baptism and confirmation are for the most part identical, including the law that parents may not be the godparents (sponsors) for confirmation. One or both parents may present the child during the rite of confirmation, but they may not be recorded as the canonical godparents. The law favors the maintenance of the baptismal godparent as the godparent for confirmation (canon 893, §2), provided that the godparent still meets all the canonical requirements, including that of living a life of faith in harmony with the duty being undertaken.

The presence of a godparent at confirmation is desirable but not strictly required. As at baptism, there can be one godparent or two (one male and one female) for confirmation. Though there is one confirmation godparent in many places, it is desirable to have two when both are the baptismal godparents and both are faithful Catholics, because the continuity of godparents is a sign of the continuity and interrelatedness of the sacraments of initiation.

♦ *John M. Huels*

Sponsors Begetting Sponsors

Saint Augustine referred to the church as a community of "Christians begetting Christians." From the very beginning, the growth of the church depended on the witness of every member. Begetting new Christians was not solely the prerogative of clergy but belonged to the entire community of Christians.

At St. Paul Parish in Englewood, Ohio, we have taken this adage of "Christians begetting Christians" one step further. We are a parish of "sponsors begetting sponsors."

That the catechumenate exists for the church and is a means of building up the entire community is the bottom line at Saint Paul's. We believe that catechumenal sponsors should be active members of the parish community. The ministry of sponsorship is one that benefits both the candidate and the sponsor. The spiritual revitalization of those serving as sponsors is so great that these persons have a need to witness to others about the power of sponsorship: the power of walking the journey of faith with a fellow sojourner. Who better to recruit potential sponsors than these Spirit-filled Christians who have themselves served so well in this ministry? And what better time to recruit sponsors than on Pentecost?

As Christians, we should trust in the power of the Spirit. The early Christians were empowered at Pentecost to go out into the world giving witness and building up the church. Pentecost today finds Christians at Saint Paul's Parish also giving witness for the purpose of building up the church.

With the cooperation of our pastor, Pentecost is the day we recruit sponsors. At each Mass, the homily centers on the responsibility each Christian has to evangelize others and build up the church today in Englewood, Ohio. As part of the homily, it is also stressed that while Pentecost is the "official" end of the formal catechumenal cycle, there is no end to the church's responsibility to spread the good news. Pentecost is a celebration of the yearly rebirth of our mission to proclaim Jesus Christ to the world. This is the time to invite others to journey with us in our Catholic Christian faith. This is the time to give serious thought to being a sponsor for these potential inquirers.

As part of the homily at each Mass on Pentecost, one neophyte and that person's sponsor address our congregation, sharing the journey of faith they have traveled together during the catechumenate. These witness talks are extremely powerful. Following this homily, "sign-up" cards printed on heavy red paper are distributed to all adult parishioners present. These cards allow persons to sign up as sponsors, to recommend other parishioners as sponsors and to list the names of potential inquirers they might know. Quiet music is played as ushers distribute and then collect these cards.

Following each Mass, parishioners are invited to stay for refreshments. Current and former sponsors, identifiable by the red carnations they wear, are present to answer any questions parishioners have. Names of potential inquirers are given to the catechumenate team for follow-up. Current sponsors call each parishioner who has expressed an interest in being a sponsor. During these phone calls, the sponsors share with the parishioner their experience, discussing the time commitment involved and trying to determine whether or not the parishioner is still interested. A member of the catechumenate team contacts those still interested in sponsorship and gives them the dates and times for the sponsor training program.

The results of our Pentecost sponsor recruitment program have been amazing. The Spirit continues to breathe new life into our church as sponsors continue to beget sponsors.

♦ *Sandra A. Chakeres*

Finding Sponsors and Godparents

What member of a catechumenate team can't tell a couple horror stories about a sponsor-catechumen relationship? Was it an initially enthusiastic sponsor who then lost interest, demonstrated by several unexplained no-shows? Was it a sponsor who became too pushy by trying to pry into the personal life of a catechumen? Was it a sponsor trying to foist devotion to some saint who allegedly appeared in a neighboring town—a devotion supposedly more important than the liturgy of the church? Was it a sponsor who took the finger-pointing, censorious stance of the John Birch Society, Opus Dei or Catholics United for the Faith? Or conversely was it a sponsor who played the cynic, agnostic or faithless critic?

Of course some of these problems can be minimized by good sponsor formation. But the point of this article is that finding can be even more crucial than forming—that recruitment is the key. Because recruitment is complex, because there's no one right way and because many teams have a strategy that works for them but may not work for others, I will set forth just a list of considerations. One consideration may be more important for a given parish than others. Some are attitudinal, some practical, some just plain common sense.

1. *Invitation System Usually Better Than Volunteer System.* Open bulletin solicitation for sponsors can lead to a lot of unnecessary problems. When sponsorship is open to everybody, the quality of the respondent's "Catholicity" cannot be assured. The motivation of the volunteer cannot be discerned easily. Ads can draw people whose qualifications are questionable. This also applies to verbal solicitation from the pulpit, "sign-up days" or any such public appeal.

   Great sensitivity is necessary in this matter. If someone other than a volunteer is chosen to sponsor a catechumen, the volunteer may not understand why he or she does not have the needed qualifications or what those qualifications are. In order to prevent hurt feelings, we suggest that the opportunity for them simply be avoided in the first place.

   These qualifications are not simply the personal preference of a team or sponsor coordinator. They are God's qualifications reflected in the mission of the parish. If the mission of a parish is strongly oriented toward good liturgical prayer, sponsors must reflect that mission in their practice, knowledge and understanding. If the mission of the parish is noted for its dedication to the causes of justice and peace, so must the sponsors be.

2. *Getting Involved and Getting To Know Parishioners.* There's no more important task for the catechumenate team, especially the sponsor coordinator, than getting to know the members of the assembly personally. For example, if the pastor recognizes after a weekend

Mass that so-and-so whom he just met at the door would make a good sponsor, he might have available in his pocket a slip to make note of it immediately.

If a sponsor coordinator realizes that a certain school board member would be a good sponsor, he or she might suggest a sabbatical, a substitute on the school board to allow the dedicated and skilled member to devote services to sponsoring for a year. That sabbatical might be very much appreciated.

Word of mouth can work well. If sensitive nonteam members know what kind of person the team wants and can make recommendations on the basis of the qualifications, a suggestion can be especially worthwhile. In that way people who the team may not know can surface.

Basic questions for us to consider are many: How can we get involved? How can we get to know the parishioners better? How can we discover the people who are so important in recruitment? Where are they? At church? At the parish council meeting? At Saturday morning kiddie sports? At choir practice? On some committee? At bingo? At school? At the golden-agers' outing? At the local hospital staff meeting or auxiliary ball?

When the pastoral or catechumenate team begin to have an eye for gifts in people, the connections between the RCIA and parish can come alive. Good sponsors are good parishioners. Teams should recognize good parishioners.

3. *Grace.* Ultimately only God can deliver a good sponsor. Prayer for fruitfulness of the recruitment task puts the responsibility where it belongs, but our prayer is a lie if we do not become God's instruments in the search. If we just sit back and wait for sponsors to drop from heaven, it won't work. Occasionally a sponsor may just happen along, but usually that is not the case. God's grace needs our cooperative effort.

   For example, Marcie may volunteer to supervise a parish dinner, but letting her just go ahead so that we can take the easy way out does not excuse the team from responsibility. The team absolutely must go the route of prayer and discernment about who might be good for what. The good of the parish is more important than the easy way out. The good of the parish is what prayer and discernment are about. What is God's way? What gifts should be used for the best benefit of the parish? And besides, maybe several people don't like to work with Marcie.

Knowing that God's grace is the final arbiter of success relieves the team not of work but of worry. According to Paul in First Corinthians, we plant and water, but God grants the increase. Openness to God's grace is our first job. Receptivity to God's way is our agenda. We may apply all our rational insight, but in the end God decides and we let go. For example, I may think Peter has all the right qualifications, but the team may consider someone else preferable for other reasons. Then it's my job to let go. Or if I think my points have not been considered adequately, I must make sure they are. Then I let go. That's all part of prayerful discernment. "Not my will but yours be done."

Prayerful discernment, which allows God's grace full reign, at least gives me peace and joy about the ministry I share in recruitment. Looking forward, I wonder in confusion. Looking backward, I see the sense of it. God's grace is like that.

4. *Good Liturgies.* The care taken in preparing and celebrating good liturgies, especially good liturgies of Christian initiation can do more than anything else to improve the quality of parishioners. Members of the assembly benefit tremendously from a well-celebrated liturgy. If the homilies hit the mark, if the music is truly liturgical, if the art and environment are appropriate, if the attitudes of the ministers are right, the assembly grows. Better parishioners appear. The whole atmosphere becomes clearer and more Catholic in the best way.

   Liturgy teams should continue to educate the assembly by example and by direct teaching. Some churches use regular blurbs in the weekly bulletin to teach about liturgy, including the RCIA: what are the scrutinies, why the dismissal of catechumens, how can today's liturgy extend into the home, how do today's lectionary selections relate to the social teachings of the church in pastoral letters and encyclicals? Inevitably this continuous teaching shows up in the quality of sponsors.

5. *Settled-in Neophytes.* This writer has found that generally neophytes do not make the best sponsors, contrary to the opinion of some. Yes, they are usually enthusiastic. Yes, they are often bursting with

generosity. But being a sponsor has about it the quality of a "Catholic way of life" that implies years of dedication that give that way of life a test. On the other hand the more mature neophytes may have some excellent ideas on people they think could become good sponsors. Ask them. You'll be surprised at the names that pop up as high-quality possibilities.

Another reason for not tapping the talents of neophytes to minister as sponsors is that it can get in the way of another call they may be experiencing, like serving in a soup kitchen, writing letters to Congress persons, supervising geriatric recreation or dedicating time and effort in their own home, building family and peacemaking.

Because our own friends in the faith are "settled-in neophytes," they, too, can be a source of names of potentially good sponsors. Of course, the purpose is not to get endless lists of people but considered lists of good parishioners. Asking a friend or neophyte for just *one* good name can place the focus on quality.

6. *Screening.* We're not testing college applicants, but various parish ministries have found solid screening to be invaluable. Nothing more than a printed sheet describing the kind of commitment sponsoring will require—covering all bases but not padding—serves well before the initial interview.

   At the initial interview, the prospective sponsor and the sponsor coordinator need to establish a healthy atmosphere of mutual respect. The terms of sponsoring and sponsor formation must be made clear, so that no one is ever surprised, for example, that mystagogy is part of the commitment, that weekly meetings and participation in specific Sunday liturgies is required. A respectful sharing of information about the particular catechumen compliments both catechumen and sponsor. Resources available for the sponsor need to be described. A picture of what is *not* expected may be helpful, especially if the coordinator feels the sponsor is anxious about the duties.

7. *Who, Me?* Just as God calls us freely and personally by name, the invitation to sponsorship should imitate that gracious surprise. When a prospect is caught by the surprise and respect of the personal invitation to minister as a sponsor, that prospect is humbled sufficiently to recognize this as God's call—nobody else's. The

feeling conveyed by the sponsor coordinator who makes the invitation is more than psychological oxygen or a "warm fuzzy." It is the same sense of awe that surrounds God's choice, God's respect, God's love. When this occurs between the sponsor coordinator and the sponsor, it just may occur again between the sponsor and the catechumen.

♦ *James A. Wilde*

Liturgical Formation of Sponsors and Godparents

A few months back, I overheard my nephew Jeremy say to his friends, "Let's play church!" As Jeremy and his friends prepared for their game, I was lost in a poignant reverie, recalling the days when his mother and I would "play church."

We would set up the piano bench in our living room, draping it with one of my mother's tablecloths. Because I was older, I was always the priest, and my sister would "serve" the Mass for me. Our Latin, honed in the parish choir, was very fine, considering the fact that we were still quite young. Necco wafers passed for communion, and we were content with our version of the Mass.

A clanging sound called me back from my daydream, and I went out to the porch to investigate the noise. There was Jeremy, banging on the metal bird feeder, transformed for the moment into a church bell for him. From all corners of the yard kids came running and in an orderly fashion took their places on the benches lined up on the porch. Once the community had assembled, "Father" Jeremy began to lead the celebration.

The thirty years that separate Jeremy and me in age witnessed a transformation in our understanding of what it means not only to *play* church but more importantly to *be* church. I didn't need any people for my church, just words; Jeremy needs the people. In my church, the priest said Mass; in Jeremy's, the people celebrate it.

The RCIA has probably helped more than anything else to effect this change in our understanding of what it means to be church. When we begin to discuss the liturgical formation of sponsors and godparents, it is important that we keep in mind that historical perspective. Many people, and your sponsors and godparents might be among them, were trained to be passive spectators at Mass. The transition into the post-Vatican II church was not always smooth, and often preparation was inadequate. We presume that by being selected to be sponsors and/or godparents they are active members of today's church, formed by their lifelong experience of worship. What a "formation process" will provide for them, therefore, is an opportunity for them to resolve lingering questions or issues related to worship, along with a process for reflecting on the experience of liturgy they have already had. This will add buoyancy to their spirit and strength to their commitment.

Of course, some of the most important elements involved in the liturgical formation of sponsors and godparents are the needs of today's church and today's catechumens. Because theirs is primarily a ministry of companionship, sponsors and godparents should be encouraged to develop the same kind of appreciation for the liturgy of the word that catechumenal communities foster. At the same time, sponsors and godparents ought to be witnesses of the importance of the liturgy in their lives.

Liturgy, derived from a Greek word meaning *service rendered for the sake of others,* is an ancient term. The fact that we use it so readily today is reflective of our altered spirituality, even though the members of the community are not always so conscious of this change.

The phrase to underscore in that definition of liturgy is "of others." At liturgy the assembly is the primary symbol of the priesthood of Jesus, and therefore each person present is engaged in serving the community—not only in the praying and singing, but especially in the support they lend by the strength of their faith. So often we hear people complain that they don't participate in worship because they "don't get anything out of it." Others attend only because they think they "owe" God at least forty-five minutes a week. Neither excuse relates even remotely to the intended purpose of liturgy. The community's gathering in prayer each week strengthens faith and unity.

There is that old scriptural dilemma about the greater value of praying to God in secret. The students regularly excuse themselves from public worship because they claim to be able to pray better when they are alone. I'm sure they are right about their prayer, but they are dead wrong about liturgy. Liturgy, or public worship, is not the place to have a cozy tryst with God, or even to develop one's private relationship with God. Liturgy is public prayer. Nurturing one's relationship with God can be a wonderful by-product of worship but not its primary purpose. These basic elements of worship and how one has experienced them as a value in life ought to be the first step in a process of liturgical formation.

Members of St. Margaret of Scotland Church had a gathering of sponsors Tuesday evening, the week before the celebration of the Rite of Acceptance into the Order of Catechumens. The meeting was facilitated by one of the previous year's sponsors and one of the parish priests. Their goal was to allow the sponsors' prejudices and presuppositions about worship to surface. It turned out to be one of the most important meetings of the year, for everyone involved was able to tell the stories of how liturgy had shaped their spirituality.

There were many stories that people shared during the course of the evening—struggles with cancer, unruly teenagers, unemployment, depression. The common denominator was the strength that the community gave to each person simply by gathering together in prayer each week. More than any abstract lectures could have provided the stories shared that evening gave testimony of the power of communal worship in the lives of the faithful.

Amid the nostalgia of "the way we were," questions surfaced that night, too—questions about the structure of the liturgy, its history, symbols that weren't quite clear. The staff left with a clearer idea of the resources they would need to provide for the sponsors, while the sponsors left with a stronger sense of the support they would be able to pass along to catechumens.

Now that the lectionary is increasingly regarded as the basic "catechetical tool" of the catechumenate, candidates have also begun to feast on the word of God. If they are to serve as valuable supports for the candidates, therefore, sponsors and godparents ought to be encouraged to develop the "warm and living love for the scriptures" the bishops at Vatican II had in mind.

Harold, a young man who was initiated three years ago, found himself wanting to return to share faith with the catechumens each Sunday. He missed that communal reflection on the word so characteristic of his days as a catechumen, and it was the one way in which he felt "let down" after his entrance into the community. His solution was to attend the 10 AM Mass and then stay for the liturgy of the word at the next Mass, leaving with the catechumens when they were dismissed to meet with them and the catechist.

Harold had eagerly anticipated the Easter Vigil and longed to be a member of the community. It came as quite a surprise to him, though, that others didn't pray as he did or seem to savor the scriptures. Harold's sponsor had moved to another state, and his godparent was uncomfortable with the idea of sharing faith and did not pay much attention to the scriptures in his own life. It was a real struggle for Harold as well as for the catechumenal team who realized that Harold's temporary solution was less than ideal. Eventually they helped to form a group of people who were willing to come together each week to reflect on the liturgy of the word and share faith.

We are not yet a people who have that "warm and living love of the scriptures" or who understand the way in which the liturgical year shapes the lives of the faithful. Because of the formative process in which the catechumens have been involved, their appreciation of these two dimensions of the Christian life is often more developed than that of their sponsors and godparents. It is important, therefore, to ensure that this development will be in tandem as much as possible so that the later needs of the neophytes can be met.

Sponsors and godparents should also have a good sense of what is involved in communal worship. Not only do they understand the elements of the eucharistic celebration, but they are also familiar with other forms of liturgical prayer, particularly the liturgy of the hours: morning and evening prayer. By encouraging catechumens to participate in other parish services and to reflect on them, a sponsor can help to foster an appreciation for other forms of worship.

Our communal worship is rooted in the express command of the Lord Jesus, "Do this in memory of me." Over the years, the words have become deeply ingrained in us because we hear them in the context of the eucharistic prayer. The familiar story of Jesus blessing and sharing the bread and wine at the Last Supper, however, occurs only in the synoptic gospels. John's gospel has another story of that famous night to relate, the washing of the feet. Jesus' command is the same, however, "Do this!" It was Jesus' intention that his followers find in him their living bread and that they go forth and be bread for one another. Besides being a celebration of service, liturgy is also very clearly a call to service directed toward each member of the community.

Too often we see Christian service in soup kitchens or shelters for the homeless as a charitable "extra" when it is actually a natural movement to go from the table to the streets. This focus can also help us to see the missionary character of our lives, whether we live that mission in the financial district, at a multinational conglomerate, in a hospital or at home raising children. Liturgy is not divorced from life; it is the "source and summit" of life.

God became human to serve and to teach us to serve. In coming to the eucharistic meal we testify to our common belief that it is the Lord Jesus who sustains and nourishes us, and we pledge that we will likewise sustain and nourish one another with the bread that is our lives.

If sponsors, godparents and catechumens see that eucharist is *the* event of the Christian people, as the remembering necessary to continue the ministry of Jesus, as the celebration of active, continuous concern for others, then we will have gone a long way toward helping to bring about the reign of God.

♦ *Julia Upton*

Adult Conversion and the Ministry of Sponsor

As a pastoral theologian, I have been interested in the stories of people's conversions for some years. This professional interest, of course, is related to a personal experience that I now associate with an adult conversion: the transition from an inherited faith that I had not really claimed as my own to a way of life that has meaning for me. The Christian writer Frederich Buechner believes that "at its heart most theology, like most fiction, is essentially autobiography." In his book, *The Alphabet of Grace*, he writes:

> Aquinas, Calvin, Barth, Tillich, working out their systems in their own ways and in their own language, are all telling us stories of their lives, and, if you press them far enough, even at their most cerebral and forbidding, you find an experience of flesh and blood, a human face smiling or frowning or weeping or covering its eyes before something that happened once. What happened once may be no more than a child falling sick, a thunderstorm, a dream, and yet it made for the face and inside the face a difference which no theology can entirely convey or entirely conceal.[1]

What happened once for me was an event of self-disclosure with a friend during a year of Clinical Pastoral Education when I was working with recovering alcoholics. It was at a time when I was feeling a great deal of confusion and chaos about my own identity and vocation. Given the courage to share my inner darkness, I discovered that my friend listened to my story, and, through his presence and compassion, said "yes" when I had been hearing only "no." In retrospect, I associate that confessional encounter with a great deal of inner serenity and healing, and in some powerful, mysterious way, with an inner conviction that God had been intimately present in our conversation. For the first time, I experienced that there was a Loving Reality that went beyond words and, at the same time, that words themselves spoken in honesty between friends, "heart speaking to heart," help reveal the healing presence of God. For the first time, too, all the theology books I had read and all the classes I had attended began to have meaning as the words and stories of others before me became a real part of my inner dialogue.

My "turning" (a traditional word for conversion)[2] led me to further research and reflection upon experiences of conversion in church history and our contemporary society. I have become convinced that inasmuch as conversion is a common, human phenomenon (although not always recognized or identified as such), it is intimately connected with the presence of loving people in our lives, that is, if it is to happen at all, *and* if it is to continue to occur.

Alcoholics Anonymous and Its Sponsor: a Paradigm

An organization, nondenominational and outside ecclesial structures, which recognizes the importance of such loving people in its own process of spiritual growth or "spiritual awakening," is Alcoholics Anonymous. The word it uses for a person who helps others experience positive change in their lives is "sponsor." My own theology of church and ministry has been greatly influenced by work with the chemically dependent and the Twelve Steps of A.A.[3]

I believe that A.A.'s understanding and practice of sponsorship has something to teach those who are involved in the implementation of the Rite of Christian Initiation of Adults (RCIA). Although the sponsor in that Christian conversion process is recognized as important, the role of the Christian sponsor is only beginning to be understood as we attempt to relate that relationship to our own cultural and personal experiences. Both those who have been asked or have volunteered to be sponsors and those who are attempting to train them have expectations, as well as anxieties and genuine bewilderment. I would propose that A.A. and its understanding of the sponsor serve as a paradigm or model from which we can learn about sponsorship in the RCIA. Bill Wilson, the cofounder of A.A., once said that A.A. is "the story of how, under God's grace, an unsuspected strength has arisen out of great weakness."[4] Any of us who take time to reflect upon our contemporary age can appreciate those words when we see that A.A.'s ongoing story is transforming not only the lives of alcoholics, but also society. As A.A. and Alanon (the association for families of alcoholics) have become known for their suggested program of recovery, more and more other self-help groups are adapting the Twelve Steps to their specific audience and needs.

Sponsorship is a relationship linked closely to the story of A.A., for that organized fellowship began with the realization that if recovery is to be ongoing, it must be shared. This conviction initially led Bill Wilson in 1935 to seek out another alcoholic when he was having second thoughts about remaining sober. Searching for someone with whom he could share his story, Bill discovered Dr. Bob Smith and in effect became his sponsor in the days immediately before and after Dr. Smith quit drinking. Because of this sharing and this relationship A.A. was born.[5]

This pattern quickly developed among the early A.A. members when some of them, even though sober for only a week or a month, began to sponsor other alcoholics who were just beginning to sober up. Their ministry of sponsorship was simple: Don't try to play God in people's lives by taking responsibility for their recovery. Simply share your story with them, be friends with them, let them begin to discover hope in a new relationship of trust and surrender with a "Higher Power" and a new fellowship that welcomes them no matter what they've felt or done. That simple yet profound ministerial method worked. From those early experiences the relationship of being a sponsor came to be formally defined in A.A. literature: "An alcoholic who has made some progress in the recovery program shares that experience on a continuous, individual basis with another alcoholic who is attempting to attain or maintain sobriety through A.A."[6]

The *Importance of Storytelling*

We can see in that definition the recognition that being a sponsor in A.A. implies some history of recovery as well as a personal commitment to the recovery program of the Twelve Steps. Implied also in that definition is that the journey of recovery is a journey shared. Thus, an A.A. sponsor is someone who is willing to share his or her compassion and wisdom with another person, a compassion and wisdom rooted in the Twelve Steps and the personal journey of each sponsor. Being a sponsor presupposes, as Bill Wilson believed, that "trying to journey alone is dangerous" and that there is great benefit in talking with another person so that direct counsel and advice can be received and given.[7]

Sponsorship also presupposes a reciprocity in the relationship: that the sponsor is in no way "better" than the one being sponsored, but only more familiar with the experience of recovery and the Twelve Steps program. As Bill Wilson expressed it in the first book of A.A. that gave the organization its name: "Never talk down to an alcoholic from any moral or spiritual hilltop: simply lay out the kit of spiritual tools for his inspection. Show him how they worked with you. Offer him friendship and fellowship."[8]

The Twelve Steps that in effect provide a structured process for ongoing change or conversion are the real guides to recovery. They bring about the fellowship of equality that exists between the sponsor and the person being sponsored for both are meant to ultimately rely on those steps—and a Higher Power. These steps are the foundation, too, for the broader community of A.A. members, what Bill Wilson called "the Fellowship of the Spirit."[9] In that fellowship, diversity is welcomed as it is in the sponsoring relationship. Just as there are differences in alcoholics' backgrounds, ages, talents, beliefs, and lengths of sobriety, so A.A. believes that there will be a variety of approaches, styles, personalities among sponsors. What seems to be a basic quality in all sponsors, however, is that they are people with whom others feel comfortable, accepted, welcomed, people with whom others can talk freely and freely share their stories. They can do so because the sponsor is willing to make his or her life, story and wisdom available on a regular basis to the person who needs the sponsor's friendship and support.

A.A.'s ministry of sponsoring and A.A.'s emphasis on the method of storytelling are intertwined. Ernest Kurtz, a historian of A.A., says that storytelling has become "the practice and indeed the essential dynamic of A.A."[10] Such storytelling includes the sharing of one's story as a form of witnessing that change is a possibility for anyone. This is done at regular group meetings or with others who may need some form of intervention when their drinking has become unmanageable.

Another form of storytelling is associated with A.A.'s Fourth and Fifth Steps: the taking of a moral inventory and sharing that self-knowledge with another human being.[11] Both forms of sharing stories help guarantee an honest and humble realism about oneself that can contribute to greater mental, emotional, physical and spiritual health.

The RCIA *and Sponsoring Relationships*

What, then, does A.A. and its understanding of the sponsor teach us, especially concerning the role of the sponsor in the Rite of Christian Initiation of Adults? Based on what we have examined above, one important concept in particular emerges: that the ministry of the RCIA sponsor needs to be "demythologized," brought down from the pedestal of exaggerated expectations and anxieties that Christian sponsors and those who train sponsors sometimes have. The sponsor's ministry and role need to be placed on a level that is more easily understood, accepted and inclusive of more people in the parish. To be a sponsor for someone on his or her journey—whether in the recovery process of the alcoholic or the conversion process of the candidate in the RCIA—is a ministry that can involve all sorts of people. It does not have to be limited to the religious "expert" or enthusiast, the professional theologian, the intellectual giant or the trained spiritual guide. If a person is simply convinced of the value of his or her experience, and desires to share that experience with another freely, that is enough with which to begin.

The foundation of an RCIA sponsor's ministry is thus a person's conviction of having something meaningful to share—and the willingness to share it. The question of freedom, however, is of utmost importance here: One shares freely *without* an enthusiasm that scares people away, *without* a form of emotional blackmail that insists either explicitly or implicitly that one's experience of faith *must be the same as someone else's*. Recalling the diversity in A.A., we as Christians and as sponsors probably need to involve ourselves more in a ministry of hospitality that welcomes a diversity of beliefs and experiences than one that tries to fit everyone into a certain mold. Another aspect of ministry is that of gratitude, an important quality for any sponsor. Born social beings, we naturally want to share experiences that we consider good and worthwhile. In our gratitude for the things and the people who have given us meaning, we want to reach out to others who are interested in our faith and fellowship or church. Becoming a sponsor is one way to share our meaningful experiences in a mature way. We celebrate our life of faith *and* acknowledge our personal and communal limitations. A.A.'s Bill Wilson expressed this underlying principle of gratitude that motivates all ministry with the simple statement, "Life gives us moments, and for those moments we give our lives."[12]

In light of A.A.'s history, its understanding of the sponsor in the recovery process, and its implicit demythologizing of that relationship, let us consider sponsorship in its most basic form: quite simply that of befriending another human being who, like ourselves, is in search of holiness. Let us look more closely at that broad ministry, one which is a part of all ministries; let us reflect on it especially in the context of our own rich heritage of Christian faith.

The Ministry of Being a Loving Friend

The theme of friendship is as old—and young—as the people of God. In our ancient Judeo-Christian myths of origins, we are told of the friendship our first parents had with a loving creator: how God called us into being, made us in God's own likeness, gave us a life and world that is fundamentally good. Before our loss of innocence, we lived in a beautiful garden and walked with God as friend (Genesis 1:26–31). The story of the Exodus tells us that the Lord, despite our willful separation and our tendency toward violence, still speaks to us as to Moses, face-to-face, "as a person speaks with a friend" (Exodus 33:11). In the poetry of the Song of Songs, we find our intimacy with God portrayed in sensual images, all reflecting the profound goodness of a friend who is also a lover (5:16). These scriptures describe the importance of friendship with God. The prophets remind our ancestors and ourselves about this friendship when we have lost sight of that relationship through obstinacy or blindness. They also remind us of the value and dimensions of friendship with one another. In the book of Proverbs, we are told that "a friend is a friend at all times" (17:17), a somewhat subtle reminder that the relationship is not only one that includes the best of times. We are also warned to be realistic about friendship: "There are friends who lead one to ruin; others are closer than brothers or sisters." (18:24)

In the gospels, the Story of a Storyteller, we find friendship an intimate part of the theology and ministry of Jesus. In his own stories he relates friendship to prayer and God's attentiveness to our needs (Luke 11:5–8). He also associates friendship with conversion, the "rejoicing among the angels of God over the repentant sinner" (Luke 15:8–10). Most importantly, he calls his followers "friends" and expects of them a ministry not of domination but of friendly service to others (John 15:12–17). He dies, accused of the worst sort of crime: "Look, a glutton and drunkard, a friend of tax collectors and sinners." (Matthew 11:19)

The Christian story, of course, does not end with accusation or death, and in the stories of those who followed Jesus we discern the importance of friends and their relationship to the Christian conversion process. What sort of conversion, for example, would St. Paul, then Saul, have experienced if he had not first (before his dramatic encounter with Christ on the road to Damascus) witnessed the eloquence and bravery of Stephen (Acts 7)? Surely Stephen's martyrdom and that of others whom Saul was persecuting must have had some effect on him: perhaps the beginning of self-doubt about his self-righteous ways; perhaps some questioning of his own ideological bias. Later, after being knocked from his horse, where would St. Paul have been without an Ananias who healed him, restored his sight, baptized him (Acts 9)? Where would Augustine have been without the prayers of his mother Monica, the mentorship of the bishop Ambrose, the companionship of Alypius, the story of the desert father Antony, the voice of a child telling him to "take up and read"?[13]

In our more recent history, what sort of person would the C. S. Lewis have become without people like Arthur Greeves who as friend acted as "father confessor"—or without colleagues like J. R. R. Tolkien and Charles Williams or students like Bede Griffiths? As Lewis admitted in the story of his own conversion, "A young man who wishes to remain a sound atheist cannot be too careful of his reading," and evidently of his friends.[14] Where would Dorothy Day have been without a Peter Maurin who became her spiritual mentor and friend, who helped give focus to her radical thought and form of ministry?[15] Her story shows that children can be identified as friends; how the birth of her child Tamar, revealed in her own "long loneliness" a loving God as friend. Without friends along the way, where would the Trappist monk Thomas Merton have been in his own discernment of vocation? What sort of life would have been his without a group of friends like Bob Lax, Ed Rice, Bob Gibney, the Hindu Bramachari; without teachers who were friends and guides like Martin Van Doren and Dan Walsh; without the instruction of Father Moore, Catherine de Hueck and the people at Friendship House? As Merton with insight writes in *Seven Storey Mountain:*

> . . . the Holy Ghost was waiting to show me the light, in his own light. And one of the chief means he used, and through which he operated, was human friendship. . . . All our salvation begins on the level of common and natural and ordinary things. . . . God brought me and a half-dozen others together at Columbia and made us friends, in such a way that our friendship would work powerfully to rescue us from confusion and misery.[16]

His journey of faith, his ascent of the mountain toward and with God, would not have happened without the loving presence of friends along the way.

Perhaps we might have trouble comparing our stories with these stories of famous men and women. These stories may seem too far removed from our seemingly ordinary day-to-day existence. But it is important for every sponsor to begin to see the *pattern* that these stories reveal. They reveal the importance of friends who make it possible for others to encounter, sometimes for the first time, the incarnate-transcendent reality we call God. And they reveal the importance of these relationships if that initial encounter is to become an ongoing way of life and not a seed that falls by the wayside.

If sponsors are to begin to see this pattern as part of their own lives and stories, if they are to begin to realize the significance of the simple ministry of friendship, let them take time to reflect. First by themselves and then with other sponsors let them ask some fundamental questions: who were (and perhaps still are) my friends? How and when did their friendship make a difference? How does it now? How could I as friend help another on his or her journey through time?

This discernment process can shed light on the ministry of being a sponsor. It can also help identify certain qualities in a sponsor that might contribute to this form of ministry. Some of these qualities, besides the gratitude, freedom and hospitality already mentioned, might be availability, compassion, openness to questions, honesty, realism, prayerfulness, patience, personal warmth, an ability to listen to and to respect others (what Carl Jung called the quality of "a truly religious person").[17] One of the most important qualities of all is that related to stories and storytelling: the willingness to share aspects of our journeys with another when and where it is appropriate. If we presuppose by now that sponsorship is a relationship of mutuality, reciprocity, equality and rapport, it necessarily follows that formal sessions and informal discussions with a sponsor are not monologues in which one person does all the talking and the other all the listening. This, of course, presupposes that the sponsor has some conviction of the value of his or her story, the growing realization that his or her journey—fragile, sinful, with moments of doubt and despair—is fundamentally a sacred one. Continuing to discern that sacredness is the task of each of us, a way of "doing theology" in its most fundamental sense: "faith seeking understanding."

These qualities can be a part of the overall ministry of friendship that the sponsor offers his or her companion in the RCIA. In reality they speak of many ministries directly related to friendship and story telling: of being a compassionate guide, an understanding mentor, a living sign of conversion, a link between the candidate and the larger community called church, a "soul friend."[18]

Conclusion

A.A. reminds us that there is no perfect sponsor and no one sponsor who combines all the qualities and ministries that could be identified. Nor should one attempt to strive for that ideal of perfection. We are, after all, neither gods nor goddesses, but brothers and sisters in Christ. The stories of conversions teach us, too, that there is no one way to encounter God (and vice-versa!) and that there is more than one way to be a sponsor or friend. We also need to become aware, as C. S. Lewis reminds us in his book, *The Four Loves,* that all friendships are ultimately gifts from God.[19] Their depth and their direction, the degrees of intimacy and rapport, cannot and should not be forced. In our lives and in our ministries we are simply called to manifest those qualities that one would naturally associate with a friend. The rest is beyond our control. What we often discover, however, is the wisdom of A.A.'s Bill Wilson (paraphrasing St. Paul): how, under God's grace, an unexpected strength has arisen out of great weakness; how those who become our friends do so, not because they are perfect, but because they share compassionately in the same human foibles as ourselves. We also may at times gratefully discover, upon reflection, how friends seem to come into our lives when we need them most, revealing the presence and care of a loving, all-accepting and forgiving friend.

♦ *Edward Sellner*

[1] Frederich Buechner, *The Alphabet of Grace* (New York: Seabury Press, 1970), 3–4.

[2] An excellent book in the theme of conversion as a "turning" or series of turnings is Emilie Griffin's *Turning: On the Experience of Conversion* (Garden City NY: Doubleday, 1980).

[3] For a thorough understanding of the Twelve Steps and A.A.'s process of "spiritual awakening," see *Alcoholics Anonymous* (New York: A.A. World Services, 1952), and *Twelve Steps and Twelve Traditions* (New York: A.A. World Services, 1952).

[4] *Alcoholics Anonymous Comes of Age* (New York: A.A. World Services, 1957), 79.

[5] The history of A.A. is a fascinating story of many conversions. See, for example, Robert Thomsen, *Bill W.* (New York: Harper & Row, 1975) and Alcoholics Anonymous, *Dr. Bob and the Good Oldtimers* (New York: A.A. World Services, 1980). Lois Wilson, wife of Bill Wilson, is the founder of Alanon. Her book *Lois Remembers* is a personal history (New York: Alanon Family Group Headquarters, 1979).

[6] *Questions and Answers on Sponsorship* (New York: A.A. World Services, 1976), 5.

[7] *Twelve Steps and Twelve Traditions,* 61.

[8] *Alcoholics Anonymous,* 95.

[9] Ibid., 164.

[10] Ernest Kurtz, *Not God: A History of Alcoholics Anonymous* (Center City MN: Hazelden, 1979), 71–74.

[11] For more information on those important steps and the ministries associated with them see my *Step Five: A Guide to Reconciliation* (Center City MN: Hazelden, 1981) and *Christian Ministry and the Fifth Step* (Center City, MN: Hazelden, 1981).

[12] Quoted in Robert Thomsen, *Bill W.,* 307.

[13] See Augustine, *Confessions,* Book 8, Chapter 12, for the story of his conversion.

[14] See C. S. Lewis, *Surprised by Joy* (New York: Harcourt, Brace and World, 1955), 191. For insight into his relationship with Arthur Greeves, see Walter Hooper, ed., *They Stand Together* (New York: Macmillan, 1979). Also, for the story of other friends, see Humphrey Carpenter, *The Inklings* (Boston: Houghton Mifflin Co., 1979) and Bede Griffiths, *The Golden String* (Springfield IL: Templegate, 1954).

[15] Dorothy Day, *The Long Loneliness* (San Francisco: Harper & Row, 1952). On page 166, she speaks of Peter as the man whose spirit and ideas came to "dominate the rest of my life."

[16] Thomas Merton, *The Seven Storey Mountain* (New York: Harcourt Brace Jovanovich, 1948), 177–78. Merton also sees the saints, in particular St. Therese of Lisieux, as friends. See especially 352–56.

[17] Carl Jung, *Psychology and Religion: West and East* (Princeton: Princeton University Press, 1973), 327–47.

[18] For an understanding of the "soul friend" or spiritual guide, see Kenneth Leech, *Soul Friend* (New York: Harper & Row, 1971) and my article "Soul Friend: Guidance on Our Sacred Journeys," *Spiritual Life* vol. 29, no. 2. Summer 1983.

[19] See C. S. Lewis, *The Four Loves* (New York: Harcourt Brace Jovanovich, 1960), especially 126–27.

Spiritual Formation of Sponsors and Godparents

Some classic treatises on the spiritual life cycle of human beings speak of the *threefold* purgative, illuminative and unitive ways. Henri J. M. Nouwen discusses another *three* movements of the spiritual life: from loneliness to solitude, from hostility to hospitality, from illusion to prayer (*Reaching Out*, 1975). Psychologist Daniel J. Levinson and others outline a *fourfold* sequence of the life cycle: childhood and adolescence, age 0–22; early adulthood, age 17–45; middle adulthood, age 40–65; late adulthood, age 60–? (*The Seasons of a Man's Life,* 1978). James W. Fowler, psychologist at Emory University, detects *six* stages of faith: intuitive-projective, mythic-literal, synthetic-conventional, individuative-reflective, conjunctive and universalizing (*Stages of Faith,* 1981; *Becoming Adult, Becoming Christian*, 1984). St. Theresa of Avila speaks of *seven* mansions of the soul's progressive growth (*The Interior Castle,* c. 1575). St. Benedict of Nursia describes *twelve* degrees of humility and *seventy-three* instruments of good works, all in progressive order reflecting the maturity of the spiritual life of the monk (*The Rule of St. Benedict*, c. 540).

Jesus the Christ did not mention stages of growth in any of his preaching. In his view, either one was growing in the reign of God or one was in sin. And Jesus' response was the same in both situations: love, compassion, mercy.

With all that said, the selection of *four* steps of spiritual growth will appear exactly what it is: arbitrary. From a liturgical, spiritual, behavioral, pastoral view, however, *four* seems to do justice both to the complexity of the topic and to its understandability by the majority of readers.

I owe the content of this chapter to Bernard Lonergan, Henri Nouwen, Scott Peck, James Fowler, St. Theresa of Avila, the author of the *Cloud of Unknowing*, Ron Lewinski, Catherine Dooley and Mark Searle. Most of all, my sources are the Bible, the documents of Vatican II and the Rite of Christian Initiation of Adults.

The four steps are:

spiritual infancy,
spiritual adolescence,
early spiritual adulthood,
mature spiritual adulthood.

Spiritual Infancy

The infant knows only the self. Daddy is part of me. The whole world is part of me. I am the center that everything else serves. When I'm hungry, my right arm Mommy feeds me. When I'm messy, my left arm changes me. If something displeases me, I cry until it is removed. I am in total control. The world is me. What I want goes.

These attitudes are completely acceptable in an infant or small child. They are not acceptable, however, later in life. Slowly growth starts. Mommy may say:

> Darling, I love you so much. I really like that brown material you produce in your diaper. I could smear it all over the wall to enjoy permanently. But could you just once for Mommy hold it back for a few minutes until I return. I love you, and I'm asking you to hold it just a little bit for me.

For the first time, the infant is asked to postpone gratification for the sake of love. The child is asked to die on the cross out of loving obedience—the first of a million crosses and resurrections that will draw the infant to mature adulthood. The child reasons:

> I will not do that. It's too uncomfortable, and, besides, Mommy has no business asking me to make that sacrifice for any reason. Hmm. She has been pretty good to me. When I'm hungry, she brings me food, and when I'm messy, she makes me feel so clean and good. Maybe just this once I'll do what she asks,. . . But only for a little while, maybe till she gets back.

The first cross borne, and when Mommy showers appreciation on the child, it is the first resurrection experienced. Death, love, life—the ingredients of spiritual growth.

There's a bit of spiritual infancy in all of us—when we mope or feel sorry for ourselves, when we refuse the cross because our immediate gratification is more important to us, when we cling tightly to our bottle or our daily 3000 calories or our petty theft or our thumbsucking for hours before the television set. Spiritual infancy is normal for infants; it is not normal for adults.

Spiritual Adolescence

The big words for adolescent spirituality are *membership* and *law*. This is the time we become part of society and groups within society. In order to become good members, we must obey society's rules. If it is a national citizenship, we must salute the flag. If it is the army, we must say "Yes, Sir." If it is the church, we must say "I believe," and come to Mass each Sunday or the consequences will be grave. If it is the Cub Scouts, we must do the tasks that earn the bear badge. If it is Weight

Watchers, we have to watch our weight. If it is school, we have to do our homework.

Spiritual adolescence is the time of socialization, the time of propaganda (in its good or bad sense). Christian adolescents are afraid of a consequence if their membership is not intact. The adjective *practicing* before *Catholic* is all important. Do I obey the laws sufficiently to be in good standing? Do I know my catechism well enough to pass the test?

This is the time to learn how to practice and pray the way the church practices and prays. It's the time to learn the prayers of the liturgy like the Sign of the Cross, the Lord's Prayer, the creed, the Gloria, the responses and acclamations, the music, morning and evening prayer. It's the time to get a firsthand familiarity with the lectionary and the meaning the church gives it. It's also the time to learn some of the nonliturgical practices and prayers like the rosary.

Frankly, most Catholics are spiritual adolescents. They've read them, but unfortunately they have still not caught on to the spirit and power of Vatican II's *Lumen Gentium, Dei Verbum, Gaudium et Spes,* and their faith still has the motivation of membership and law. Just as frankly, many preachers, pastors and priests are still reluctant to help people move past spiritual adolescence into spiritual early adulthood, for reasons not the least of which are financial. Empty pews mean empty collection baskets.

Early Spiritual Adulthood

Rationality is the big word in early spiritual adulthood. Normally it begins in the late teens or early twenties, a time at which the young adult begins trying to "make sense" of the laws and practices that have been handed down. It is not uncommon for college-age students to move through a period of agnosticism, Marxism or a psychological approach to life. Through these approaches the student tries to find personal meaning through intellectual, cognitive ways that differ greatly from those of parents, church, government or other institutions.

Practically it may mean that the young adult stops going to church, becomes involved in a quasi-scientific practice like transcendental meditation or dianetics. The young adult can just as easily give himself or herself sports, hard sciences and highly creative work. The spiritually young adult may argue that there is more peace and meaning Sunday mornings on the golf course than there is in church. Sincere dedication is not at all unknown to the spiritually young. Norman Vincent Peale or Robert Schuller appeal to the spiritually young adult. Insight and rationality are equivalent to salvation. *Meaning for me* may even suggest the psychiatrist's couch, group therapy, dream analysis, intensive journaling, advanced study or, at times, mind-altering drugs.

The frequent movement away from church is the reason churches have not successfully encouraged people to grow into this step, necessary and worthy though it is. It means less money for the church. But for the individual it may mean poetry, art, music, liberation, growth, responsibility. Many professional people are at this step. It is a definite step beyond spiritual adolescence and a necessary prerequisite to spiritual maturity. There can be no spiritual maturity without this step.

Mature Spiritual Adulthood

Image and *symbol* are what the spiritually mature adult lives. The spiritually mature adult is a *community builder* and a *totally other* person. As the infant draws everything to itself, the mature adult lets go of everything to serve others. Mature adults trade in their psychiatrist's couch for a spiritual director. They have found themselves and no longer need to grasp and pull at gratification or identity. They turn outwards and reach to help others for meaning in life.

They tend to move back to the churches, not because they are concerned about membership or are afraid of consequences but rather because that is where the people are who need community building, consolation and healing. They can move as easily into Judaism, Buddhism or Christianity. Beyond denominational lines, their interest is more in helping others, no matter who they are. Spiritually mature adults are motivated by symbols and images. The eucharist for them may be food enough. The holy name in the centering prayer, the prayer of quiet or the liturgy may be a source of such great hope that it serves them to heroic ministry. Frequently apostolic works of peace and justice follow close suit to the prayer of the mature adult. The Sign of the Cross, the Lord's Prayer recited slowly, the Jesus

Prayer—all these are anchors for the spiritually mature adult. They energize, they release power, they offer peace.

They live from the lectionary—the stories and words, the biblical images of God's love and justice. The people in the stories and the words on their lips—these give daily life to the spiritually mature.

He or she may tap this power and love through the bread that comes down from heaven, through the word of life that comes forth from God's lips, by breathing in and breathing out the air God provides to animate all the living, by intensive journaling to connect solidly with the one inside—the dream giver, the reality maker, the creator—through physical self-discipline, so that the peace of God's reign pervades every human heart. In short, the word discipline, related to Christ's death, and in turn related to obedience unto death on a cross—that is where we become transformed by God's love to become the risen person full of joy, prosperity and wholeness.

Practical Observations

Catechumens and candidates should be encouraged by their sponsors and godparents to start with membership in the church, spiritual adolescence as described above. Sponsors or godparents should not rush a catechumen to step forward too rapidly. God converts; we do not. Rather, helping candidates learn the practice and prayers of public worship is our most important task. Catechumens should learn about our fasting, about our music, about Catholic practice and belief in the eucharist long before the emphasis is placed on mature spiritual adulthood. There's time enough for that. If the sponsor is not a mature adult, no pretense should be given. Truth and growth are far more productive for all than any other alternative.

In some things the student will have surpassed the master. That is all right. What a great credit to the master! If that is the case, the sponsor or godparent should waste no opportunity in his or her own personal growth. In spiritual formation, everybody wins.

The reason for maturity in the first place is love and unity. The fully mature human being is one with God, one with fellow human beings and one with the whole universe. The mature person can experience the connectedness of creation and will take responsibility to help that connectedness, the responsibility for inching in the reign of God, a just world, peace on earth and love.

♦ *James A. Wilde*

Forming Sponsors and Godparents in the Ministry of Peace and Justice

People who become godparents or sponsors today may well have confusing thoughts and feelings about their responsibilities, particularly as these touch upon the mission of the church. Many potential sponsors will not even give a thought to this dimension of their responsibilities unless they are given help.

There are considerable environmental factors that militate against apostolic formation. The very word *apostolic,* which carried the freight of the social dimension of the Christian life a generation ago, is no longer a powerful word in Catholic circles. This is unfortunate, because we have no new symbol that equally evokes the idea of Christian life that is oriented beyond the Christian community itself. *Apostolate* and *Catholic action* have given way to *ministry* and *peace and justice.* This is not the place to describe and analyze reasons for these shifts in language. The new terms represent much that is positive. Our task is to work within this new frame of reference to help sponsors and godparents, as well as ourselves, understand well our vocation to participate in the redeeming and transforming work of Christ.

It is not only our notions and experience of the church and its mission that have changed. Our experience of the earth itself, and of the world, that is, of the earth as socially organized, has changed profoundly. Much of this reality is so overwhelming and painful that we may often find ourselves shrinking from the data that describe it. If we recognize this temptation to avoidance in ourselves, we can be more compassionate towards those who shy away from social issues because they simply do not know how to cope adequately. They, and we, may also have had some negative experience of a justice and peace methodology that used methods of moral coercion that unfortunately left people feeling overwhelmed, guilty, angry and finally indifferent.

Still, it is important, even necessary, to be attentive to the situation in which we actually live. What characterizes it is a new level of interdependence that has great consequences for the way we conduct ourselves as Christians. To cite only one example, because of our dependence on fossil fuels, our relationship to people of the Middle East may be more vital than our relationship to some of our neighbors who live on the same street. The close linkages that are the consequence of technology make us vulnerable to each other's actions and also responsible for each other's lives.

It is not only the fact of interdependence that fundamentally conditions our apostolic formation. There are also the realities of massive evil and suffering that characterize our century. The fact that our dealing with these realities has been less than adequate should not be used as an excuse for escape. Rather, the enormity of the problem can be seen as a cry to God for mercy, particularly for the merciful grace that will draw us more deeply into the mystery of the redemption of the world. In the opening lines of Vatican II's *Pastoral Constitution on the Church in the Modern World* we find a perfect expression of the posture that should be our own. "The joys and the hopes, the griefs and the anxieties of the people of this age, especially those who are poor or in any way afflicted, these too are the joys and hopes, the griefs and anxieties of the followers of Christ."

Central to a vital apostolic spirituality is the personal realization that the church is missionary by her nature, that is, that the church exists for all people, not only for her own members. This does not mean that the direct goal of all apostolic activity is to bring every individual person into the church; it does mean that the church, by the way it lives in society, is meant to be a sign of the loving, redeeming activity of her Lord, Jesus Christ.

It may very well be that those who are preparing to be godparents or sponsors have not made their own this vision and understanding of the mystery of Christ and the church. Even those who have kept pace with the deepened self-understanding of the church since the Second Vatican Council will need help in drawing out the implications of their understanding of Christ and the church.

Here, the renewed accent on the church as a community of disciples can be of immense benefit. Without losing anything of the emphasis on responsibility for the transformation of the social order, the church as a community of disciples establishes apostolic activity on the only adequate foundation, that is, on a growing union of mind and heart with the mind and heart of Christ.

In their 1983 pastoral letter, "The Challenge of Peace," the bishops of the United States devote the entire fourth section to the notion of church as a community of disciples in the United States. They begin by quoting from Pope John Paul's encyclical, "Redeemer of the Human Race."

> Membership in that body {the church} has for its source a particular call, united with the saving action of grace. Therefore, if we wish to keep in mind this community of the people of God, which is so vast and so extremely differentiated, we must see first and foremost Christ saying in a way to each member of the community: "Follow me." It is the community of the disciples, each of whom in a different way—at times very consciously and consistently, at other times not very consciously and consistently—is following Christ. This also shows the deeply "personal" aspect and dimension of this society.
>
> — *"The Challenge of Peace,"* 274

The bishops use this passage to introduce their own teaching on "the implications of being a community of Jesus' disciples in a time when our nation is so heavily armed with nuclear weapons and is engaged in a continuing development of new weapons together with strategies for their use" (275). The implications strike this reader, at least, as astonishing, for the bishops go on to talk about martyrdom. Given the position of this passage in a pastoral letter that was discussed and revised over a period of several years and that was intended as a teaching document, the following passage describing the way of Christian life deserves and needs careful study.

> To be disciples of Jesus requires that we continually go beyond where we now are. To obey the call of Jesus means separating ourselves from all attachments and affiliations that could prevent us from hearing and following our authentic vocation. To set out on the road to discipleship is to dispose oneself for a share in the cross (cf. John 16:20). To be a Christian, according to the New Testament, is not simply to believe with one's mind, but also to become a doer of the word, a wayfarer with and a witness to Jesus. This means, of course, that we never expect complete success within history and that we must regard as normal even the path of persecution and the possibility of martyrdom. (276)

We can document what the bishops say by recalling contemporary Christian martyrs: Archbishop Oscar Romero, Jean Donovan, Ita Ford, Maura Clark, Dorothy Kazel and many others whose names are unknown to us, who have died because of their faithful service to and solidarity with their poor brothers and sisters. We recall, too, the names of martyrs of the 1930s and 1940s whose stories are becoming an important chapter of our Christian heritage, such persons as Franz Jaegerstaetter, the Austrian peasant who was beheaded because he refused to serve in the Nazi army, and Fr. Rupert Mayer, SJ, apostle of the poor in wartorn Munich who was beatified in 1987.

The 1985 pastoral letter of the U.S. bishops, "Economic Justice for All: Catholic Social Teaching and the U.S. Economy," like the earlier letter on peace and war, establishes its moral teaching on the vision of church as a community of disciples. Here, the applications are in areas that touch immediately the daily lives of all Catholics, for no one lives outside an economy, though not all experience economic life the same way. It will take the U.S. church years to appropriate the strong teaching of this letter, which is organized around the biblical themes of creation, covenant and community. In developing these themes the bishops' letter explains and insists upon a "preferential option for the poor." Facing up to the requirements of justice for those who are the victims of unjust systems and structures is a central demand of the Christian life. In the bishops' own words:

> The biblical vision of creation, covenant and community, as well as the summons to discipleship, unfolds under the tension between promise and fulfillment. Although ultimate realization of God's plan lies in the future, Christians in union with all people of goodwill are summoned to shape history in the image of God's creative design and in response to the reign of God proclaimed and embodied by Jesus. (53)

The landmark pastoral letters of our U.S. bishops did not arise out of nowhere. They are powerful teaching documents precisely because they are grounded within the tradition of Catholic social thought. Catholic social teaching has developed steadily over the past century since the seminal encyclical of Pope Leo XIII, "On the Reconstruction of the Social Order" (1891). Though this body of teaching, shaped over almost a century, has not yet found an adequate place in Catholic higher education, including seminary education, elements of its teaching do find their way into curricula and catechesis. Certainly this teaching should be an essential part of sacramental preparation.

It is important to have an overall grasp of the main lessons of this body of teaching. In a very useful book, *Our Best Kept Secret: The Rich Heritage of Catholic Social Teaching,*[1] the authors identify what they consider the ten major lessons of Catholic social teaching as the following:

1. Link of religious and social dimensions of life
2. Dignity of the human person
3. Option for the poor
4. Link of love and justice
5. Promotion of the common good
6. Political participation
7. Economic justice
8. Stewardship
9. Global solidarity
10. Promotion of peace

Our Best Kept Secret also specifies some shifts in attitude of the church towards the world, shifts that are especially discernible since Vatican II. The first is a shift from an attitude of no responsibility for political life to an assault on political apathy. This is especially pronounced in Pope Paul VI's letter, "A Call to Action," written in preparation for the 1971 Synod that dealt with justice in the world. It was that synod that laid down the principle that "action on behalf of justice and participation in the transformation of the world fully appear to us as a constitutive dimension of the preaching of the gospel, or in other words, of the church's mission for the redemption of the human race and its liberation from every oppressive situation." This important sentence can be used as well to illustrate a second shift, from an accent on the world as a place of danger and temptation, to an accent on responsibility for the humanization of the world. In his encyclical "On Human Work," Pope John Paul II teaches that people can rightly see themselves as contributing to God's creative work through their labor. This leads to an attitude that is a far cry from disdain for the earthly project.

Quite clearly, a lifetime is not long enough to acquire a thorough understanding of the contemporary social teaching of the church. What the situation calls for is a methodology that will keep us on the path, keep us moving in the right direction, help us develop as ever more faithful members of the community of disciples. For that methodology to be more than a set of techniques it must include a grasp of the structure and dynamics of the social order—and social disorder.

We need to understand that the institutions that make up the societal context of our lives embody values. Social institutions are not neutral. Economic institutions, for example, can, and in many cases do, foster greed. Cultural institutions, too, can foster both our best and our worst tendencies. Much of our advertising, for example, strongly abets the innate tendency toward selfishness, overindulgence and lack of respect and concern for natural resources and the wholesomeness of the environment.

Happily, there are also institutions that embody grace, though these are not so easily found and require constant investments of generosity. Think, for example, of Alcoholics Anonymous and of the redemptive role it has played in many lives. Within the church as a community of disciples, institutions of grace should abound and flourish. Where they are weak or lacking, the situation awaits the commitment of informed and mature Christians. Many of the pages of church history are those that tell of just such Christians who were sensitive to the social needs of their day. They were alert to what modern Catholic social teaching calls the "signs of the times."

The phrase "signs of the times" can be found in the New Testament. Its present use stems from Pope John XXIII and from the Second Vatican Council. In his encyclical "Peace on Earth" (1963) Pope John specified particular widespread conditions in the world that indicated where there was an opening for further humanizing action. The council, particularly in the *Pastoral Constitution on the Church in the Modern World*, continued this methodology and it has now become a generally practiced theological method. What this means is that we look to experience, especially widespread social experience, as the locus for God's action and call in our lives. To give only one example, and one that comes as a surprise to many people, John XXIII has this to say in "Peace on Earth":

> It is obvious to everyone that women are now taking a part in public life. This is happening more rapidly perhaps in nations with a Christian tradition, and more slowly, but broadly, among peoples who have inherited other traditions or cultures. Since women are becoming ever more conscious of their human dignity, they will not tolerate being treated as inanimate objects or mere instruments, but claim, both in domestic and in public life, the rights and duties that befit a human person. (41)

Once the main lines of Catholic social teaching are grasped, we are on our way to appreciating a programmatic approach to the apostolic formation of adult Christians and here, specifically, of sponsors and godparents. In many years of teaching and writing about the social dimension of the Christian vocation, I have found the following eight modes of activity useful for encouraging others as well as myself to keep growing in this essential dimension of Christian life. Each of us will find her/his own preferred mode or modes, depending on particular gifts and circumstances. Appreciating all eight as genuine modes of apostolic action can help us to affirm in others those ways that may not be our own preferred way of serving. At the same time, we can be motivated to continue to develop the ways that best correspond to our own gifts and possibilities. The ways:

Reminding. We need to keep our poor and suffering brothers and sisters on the agenda. The voiceless need to find in us a voice. Short excerpts from Catholic social teaching in parish bulletins (such as those found in *The Pastorals on Sundays*, Liturgy Training Publications), letters to the editor, these and hundreds of other ways depend only on our understanding and our commitment.

Interpreting. This is an important step beyond reminding. Interpreting shows causes, relationships; it helps answer the "how" and "why" questions and places facts that could otherwise be overwhelming in a meaningful context. Interpreting can keep people from feeling paralyzed by their responsibilities. To grow in this area, there is no substitute for serious ongoing study of the major documents of the social teaching of the church. Positive attitude towards this teaching is not enough. We need to own it.

Advocating. Apostolic formation does not end in a set of intellectual conclusions, but in a way of life. A community of disciples cannot be content with understanding social issues. Like Jesus, we must be actively on the side of the poor, actively on the side of all those whose dignity is denied. Here, joining such a group as Pax Christi[2] or Bread for the World[3] will enable the individual and the Christian community to transform desires for peace and justice into effective action, along with thousands of other committed persons.

Resisting. A strong and public "no" to evil is the other side of advocacy. To find the best ways to say no demands ongoing personal and group discernment. If we shrink from this mode of action ourselves, at the very least we can understand its place and affirm those of our community of disciples who act generously in resisting institutional evil. In every generation there have been Christians who have gone to jail and prison as the price of their resistance. For most of us it is easier to admire these persons at a safe distance than it is to imitate them.

Caring. The world is meant to be home for everyone, yet ours is a century of the homeless in our own cities, of millions of refugees, of old people hidden away, of the unemployed avoided in the hope that they will disappear. The Christian community has a special vocation to make God's love visible and tangible as Jesus did and as those we especially honor in our communion of saints have done throughout the ages.

Community building. Deep in our Western cultural heritage is a strong streak of individualism. Deep in our Christian heritage is the central mystery of communion with God through communion with each other. Today, especially, we need to invest in building a community that sustains its members as we grow together in Christian response to all those who are marginalized. These include entire classes and even countries exploited by and for others. Social problems look very different when we see them in the context of Jesus' example and teaching about community.

Vision. "Where there is no vision people perish." American pragmatism too easily leads us into the trap of thinking that no problem is beyond our ability to solve. We like to think narrowly in terms of ways and means. This is not an attitude that will help develop a strong Christian social spirituality. We need to take time to enter the mysterious dimension of reality, to celebrate the presence of God, to mourn the denials of God's love as these denials destroy the lives of God's beloved children. Those who take the risks of contemplation undertake an essential work in the social ministry of the church. The call to see, to imagine the possible, what Jesus called the reign of God, is addressed to each of us in unique ways. Some among us will excel in the ability to envision. All of us need to appreciate and encourage contemplatives with a social conscience, even while we tend carefully our own contemplative gifts.

Prayer. Prayer that is informed by faithful action will in turn form us for continuing action on behalf of peace and justice. To let the world into our prayer is deeply disturbing, and should be. If we are not adept at integrating prayer and social action, we can begin simply by reflecting on the front page of the daily newspaper from the perspective of Jesus' teaching in Matthew 5—6. Another form of prayer is to reflect on the eight modes of apostolic activity enumerated here as these are found in the gospel accounts of the public ministry of Jesus.

Finally, none of the above will work without some support group or support structure. In the beginning, this may be as small as one other person with whom we share our efforts. The dynamics of the situation will almost invariably bring about some kind of expansion. To those who say they cannot find such a support community there is an answer. Find it. This is precisely what is happening throughout the church today, as men and women respond to the call to participate in God's transforming action in the world.

♦ *Mary Evelyn Jegen*

[1] Michael J. Schultheis and others, *Our Best Kept Secret: The Rich Heritage of Catholic Social Teaching,* 3rd ed. (Washington DC: Center of Concern and Orbis Books, 1988).

[2] Pax Christi USA is a branch of the only international Catholic peace movement. Its purpose is to work for peace among all people, always witnessing to the peace of Christ. It does this through a program of prayer, study and action on selected social issues. Address: 348 East Tenth Street, Erie PA 16503.

[3] Bread for the World is a Christian citizens' lobby on hunger and related issues. Address: 802 Rhode Island Avenue, NE, Washington DC 20018.

Hispanic Traditions of Padrinos and Madrinas

Infant baptisms occur all the time even though adult baptism is the normative practice of the church according to the Rite of Christian Initiation of Adults. Engrained deeply within hispanic Catholic parents is the desire to baptize their infant child as soon as *padrinos* and *madrinas* (godparents) can be chosen for the baptism and the fiesta afterwards. Choosing the right padrinos (a word used generically for padrinos *and* madrinas) can take some time, even years in some cases.

The RCIA is being tailored, in some areas, to fit the living reality of the hispanic community. Many hispanics though baptized are not evangelized, that is, they are nominal Christians living unreflected gospel lives. The seeds of faith are deep within them. Provided with care and catechesis these seeds are able to blossom into lives of healthy Christian commitment. The tradition of padrinos is an important part of such commitment.

Recently among hispanic youth, we discover many who have not received any of the sacraments of initiation or have received only baptism. Now in their mid-teens or late teens they find themselves in the embarrassing situation of having to receive confirmation and eucharist. The embarrassment comes because confirmation and eucharist are considered kid's sacraments. It seems as if they must have done something wrong in not receiving them sooner and are now being punished.

The RCIA is not a catchall for every catechetical or evangelical effort in a parish. It is not necessarily a more personal approach for preparing children for first communion. It should be common knowledge by now that the RCIA is not a program or course of studies. It is a way of life, a process of discernment, a path of conversion, an implantation into the holy people of God, an encounter with God. It demands that people, with all their humility, become involved.

The RCIA needs to be incarnated into the life of a person who seeks the Lord, into the parish community that serves the Lord, into the world that needs the Lord. This incarnation in our case presumes a hispanic cultural or religious encounter that is clearly recognized as hispanic.

Our purpose here is to offer one suggestion as to what form this hispanic incarnation of the RCIA might take. It stresses the lifelong process rather than a one-, two- or three-year model. This process is celebrated in religious moments, both sacraments and popular religious customs. These customs intersect sacramental encounters by the fact that sacraments are either directly involved or at least strongly related to the tradition.

Dionisio Borobio in his book, *Proyecto de Iniciación Cristiana,* (editorial Descleé de Brouwer, Bilboa, 1980) also suggests that the RCIA be a lifelong process that begins with the newborn infant and moves to the times of serious decisions, the early 20s, and is fulfilled in a life of service (ministry). This process placed within the religious, sacramental, cultural moments of the hispanic family would be the incarnation of the RCIA into *this* particular family.

Central to the sacramental moments already mentioned is the role of the padrino y madrina, (godfather/godmother). The roles traditionally establish a family relationship between padrino/madrina, godchild and with the compadres (parents of the child). It is a relationship that has certain rights and obligations attached to it. It extends for life. In many cases it means providing for the welfare of the child as he/she grows to adulthood.

Joaquin, Alejandro and the RCIA

Sponsorship within the RCIA means giving not just personal testimony as to the worthiness of the candidate but testimony by the way the sponsor already lives. Blending this testimony with the family bonds of the compradazco (godparent) relationship could mean, quite literally, having a lifelong mentor, companion and guide. Could we not consider this a ministry? Would it not rekindle the gospel value of testimony within the compadre system? There are difficulties inherent, such as family mobility, ongoing formation, community acceptance, but granted all this, the process suggests a joining of religious practices and family patterns into one journey. How might this ideally look? Perhaps a very short story will illustrate this best.

Two-month-old Joaquin was the pride and joy of his parents, José y María, when he was born. Today he was their reason for anxiety and tension. He started to cry and scream almost immediately upon entering the church. Some superstitious people said that this crying was the devil's work, meaning the child didn't like God's house. The baby kept providing enough reasons why he needed to be here with all the fuss and fury he was making.

Father John, a kindly, tolerant and experienced cleric, smiled patiently and tried to raise his voice without seeming to be irritated. Just prior to the pouring of water, the "miracle" happened. Being instructed to hand the child over to his padrinos for the actual baptism, the infant stopped crying almost instantly when embraced by his padrinos Alejandro y Juana. This only confirmed the fact to José and María that they had chosen well. They remember spending time considering different couples, but none showed themselves equal to the love, simplicity and piety that these two people demonstrated to them. When they introduced Joaquin at the church weeks before for the traditional Presentación del Niño, the priest signed their child with the oil of catechumens and then entrusted him to Alejandro and Juana to protect, instruct and live with them as members of their own family. Now, even though Joaquin didn't understand what was going on, the family was sure that padrinos would tell him all about this day.

The boy grew and as he did so did the appreciation and affection of the compadres for one another. Joaquin's first communion was a family decision. They waited until he was a bit older than the customary seven. The reason seemed obvious—the boy couldn't quite grasp the moment. Even though he knew prayers and some basic facts, his padrinos and parents wanted him to grow up more and appreciate better what they felt and believed to be such an important part of their lives. Eucharist would be a family experience. The day arrived in all its splendor. Surrounded by these four adults and his younger brothers and sisters, Joaquin boldly said, "Amen!"—sure of his response.

Joaquin's struggles as a teenager sometimes terrified him, though he kept an easy smile on his handsome face. "He looks more and more like his grandfather, of all people," said his parents, grateful that he didn't imitate his grandfather's penchant for travel and adventure. Joaquin stopped going to church during these years. This was a disappointment to everyone, but he thought, "I've got to decide for myself. I pray, I love God, I've just got. . . ." All the excuses and objections poured out each time he was asked about his behavior. The decision to leave him alone was a decision by his godparents not to abandon him, but rather to leave themselves open to him and his life.

And so it happened, one ugly day when the cold wind seemed to rip through his winter jacket. With his head down, challenging nature's bitterness, he walked into four men about his age, with stern faces, frozen eyes and cold stares. "What's your hurry?" they asked. The question seemed completely illogical given the force of the wind, the temperature and the situation. Joaquin recognized them as being part of the 2-2 Club who were enemies of anyone from "26th Street," which is where he happened to live. "No sweat, bro," "just passing through," "just going to visit my lady." The tenseness of the moment easily made the cold a forgotten subject. Joaquin thought many things but not as much as, "What have I done to deserve this?" The 2-2s closed in, distorting everything to appear to be a meeting of good friends. If it weren't for the passing of a patrol car, things could have ended differently than just the warning to remember to stay where you belong and then the fast disappearance of all involved.

Joaquin changed his direction to his padrinos' house. In telling the story of what had happened, he suddenly found himself talking more and more about himself. It was like not being able to control himself anymore, he just talked and talked. Alejandro patiently listened, knowing the importance of this moment. It ended as he had hoped and so often prayed. "It's time to decide," Joaquin said. "Help me."

Joaquin's decision was ratified in his confirmation. He chose the name Samuel and became involved in his parish youth group. Alejandro definitely noticed a change in his godson's attitude about the church. As he stood next to him in line to receive the bishop's anointing, he realized that Joaquin was almost eye-to-eye with him. He filled out his adolescent frame and now stood as a young man. "Our lives are coming to fulfillment," Alejandro thought as they approached the bishop.

Years passed. Never had anyone thought that fulfillment would have meant *this*. But this was the day. It seemed so impossible and yet so right. Joaquin's interest and concern for other young people had turned into an earnest desire to help others. The more he did, the more he enjoyed himself, and now his joy was overflowing. He was to be ordained a priest today. Surrounded by his family, he was presented to the bishop. His padrinos had the privilege of placing the stole upon his shoulders. Tears ran down their faces that day, tears and smiles all joined together.

There were many more great moments between the families and Joaquin. There were stories of secret childhood pranks about which the adults never knew. There were old jokes that still made everyone laugh. There were stories of painful remembrances about the deaths of Alejandro's wife and Joaquin's little sister. There were stories of their lives that kept them all together. Through them all Alejandro had stayed close in heart and spirit to his godson.

The years continued to fly by. "Why did this chapter have to be written, Lord?" prayed Joaquin's padrino, as he tied his tie and looked—rather stared—at himself in the mirror. His heartache showed not only in his face but across his shoulders and over his entire body. The years passed so quickly and aged him so wonderfully.

But now those years pressed down upon him all at once. Joaquin had died.

At the funeral Alejandro carried his godson again, remembering those first days some sixty-eight years ago, remembering the rough-and-tumble of the playground and the hand-in-hand walks of autumn, remembering his godson's hand upon his hand in blessing after ordination, remembering their heart-to-heart openness about life with God. "And so it is Lord, you leave me with my memories of this man."

"Help me, help his parents and the rest of us who hurt so terribly as we bring him home to you," spoke Alejandro on the first day of the *Novenario.* He would lead the prayers and rosary for Joaquin during these nine days. He would arrange the Mass that would conclude it all. He would continue to be padrino to his godson. "Oremos . . ." he prayed.

The compadrazco (padrino/madrina) relationship can be an RCIA ministry. It is a style of life that can celebrate key cultural moments, tempered with evangelical-style reflection, as moments of growth in prayer and faith. Nothing occurs in a vacuum or as a singular event. They are all woven together into the fabric of a lifetime. This fabric can have the definite color and hue of the hispanic community.

♦ *Arturo Perez*

Bibliography

Austin, Gerard. *The Rite of Confirmation: Anointing with the Spirit.* New York: Pueblo Publishing Co., 1983. Excellent discussion of oils, anointing and other confirmation symbols.

Barbernitz, Patricia. *RCIA Team Manual.* New Jersey: Paulist Press, 1986. Good team manual approach.

Carey, Patrick W., editor. *American Catholic Religious Thought: The Shaping of a Theological and Social Tradition.* Illuminating collection of the thoughts of such American Catholic religious leaders as John Ireland, Dorothy Day, Virgil Michel and John Courtney Murray.

Caroluzza, Thomas J. "The Catechumenate, Journey toward Renewal." *Journal of the Liturgical Conference* 4, no. 1 (1983): 45–49. RCIA enables the congregation to begin to share its faith with each other and with newcomers. This is a story of one parish and how the implementation of RCIA led to total parish renewal.

Cunningham, Lawrence S. *The Catholic Faith: An Introduction.* New York: Paulist Press, 1987. *The best* doctrinal introduction to Catholicism, reflecting Sacred Scripture, the history of theology, Vatican II, ecumenical perspectives and an uncanny way of getting to the kernel of the real issues.

_______________. *The Catholic Heritage: Martyrs, Ascetics, Pilgrims, Warriors, Mystics, Theologians, Artists, Humanists, Activists, Outsiders and Saints.* New York: Crossroad, 1983. Touching descriptions of a broad variety of male and female leaders who found a home for themselves in Catholicism.

_______________. *Faith Rediscovered: Coming Home to Catholicism.* New York: Paulist Press, 1987. Special questions of people who seek full communion in the church. Excellent.

Day, Dorothy. *The Long Loneliness: An Autobiography.* San Francisco: Harper and Row, 1952. An example of a mature woman in the 20th century church; giving and reflective.

DeGidio, Sandra. *RCIA: The Rites Revisited.* Minneapolis: Winston Press, 1984. Creative reworking of the rites along with some additional rituals.

Duggan, Robert, editor. *Conversion and the Catechumenate.* New York: Paulist Press, 1984. Articles by Dick, Dunning, Moseley, Cameli, Braxton,

Searle, Duffy from several perspectives on conversion. Notable are Dunning's and Braxton's.

Dujarier, Michel. *The History of the Catechumenate: The First Six Centuries.* New York: Sadlier, 1979. One of the finest studies of the history of the catechumenate of the early church. Catechists, catechumenate directors, sponsor coordinators, pastors, pastoral associates and religious educators need this book.

______________. *The Rites of Christian Initiation: Historical and Pastoral Reflections.* New York: Sadlier, 1979. The rites in the light of their patristic, historical and secondary sources. Suggestions for pastoral application.

______________. "Sponsorship." *Adult Baptism and the Catechumenate.* Edited by Johannes Wagner. *Concilium* 22 (1981): 45–50. Well-written but poorly translated early history of sponsorship by an authority on the subject from Cotonou (Benin), West Africa.

Dunning, James B. *New Wine: New Wine Skins.* New York: Sadlier, 1981. Now a classic. Reflection on the personal and ecclesial dimensions of the RCIA.

Dunning, James and William Reedy, editors. *Christian Initiation Resources Reader.* 4 volumes. New York: Sadlier, 1984. Selection of the best articles from Sadlier's older *Christian Initiation Resources* series.

Fowler, James W. *Becoming Adult, Becoming Christian.* San Francisco: Harper and Row, 1984. Updating of the more famous volume of 1981.

______________. *Stages of Faith: The Psychology of Human Development and the Quest for Meaning.* San Francisco: Harper and Row, 1981. Pioneer work on a six-stage lifespan model; convincing and sophisticated with regard to behavioral models.

Groeschel, Benedict J. *Listening at Prayer.* New York: Paulist Press, 1984. Excellent, clear guide for listening to life, listening to the word, listening at liturgy and preparing for contemplation.

Hammarskjöld, Dag. *Markings.* New York: Alfred A. Knopf, 1966. Example of journaling.

Harris, Maria. *Teaching and Religious Imagination: An Essay in the Theology of Teaching.* The thoughts of one of America's finest religious teachers on the use of the imagination and the role of incarnation, revelation, grace, and re-creation in teaching, as well as a comparison of pedagogical and artistic models of teaching.

Henderson, Joseph L. *Thresholds of Initiation.* Middletown CT: Wesleyan University Press, 1967.

Huck, Gabe, Gordon Lathrop and Gail Ramshaw, editors. *An Easter Sourcebook: The Fifty Days.* Chicago: Liturgy Training Publications, 1988. A mystagogical prayer and reflection guide that no neophyte or sponsor can do without. Recommended without reservation.

Huck, Gabe and Mary Ann Simcoe, editors. *A Triduum Sourcebook.* Chicago: Liturgy Training Publications, 1983. For catechumenal retreat during the Triduum.

Kavanagh, Aidan. *Confirmation: Origins and Reform.* New York: Pueblo, 1988. Cogent argument for the origins of confirmation as dismissal formula. Excellent book. Challenges almost all other theories with astute clarity.

______________. "Confirmation: A Suggestion from Structure," *Worship* 58 (1984): 386–95. Preview article of *Confirmation: Origins and Reform.*

______________. "Critical Issues in the Growth of the RCIA in North America." *Catechumenate: A Journal of Christian Initiation* 10 (March 1988): 10–21. Magnificent description of the direction the RCIA must turn at this point.

______________. "The Presentations: Creed and Lord's Prayer." *Catechumenate: A Journal of Christian Initiation* 9 (July 1987). A creative and powerful commentary on the Rite of the Presentation of the Creed and the Rite of the Presentation of the Lord's Prayer. Suggestions for celebration of the rites.

______________. *The Shape of Baptism: The Rite of Christian Initiation.* New York: Pueblo, 1978. A classic.

Keifer, Ralph A. "Christian Initiation: The State of the Question." *Worship* 48, no. 7: 392–404. Excellent, far-reaching, visionary.

Kemp, Raymond. *A Journey in Faith.* New York: Sadlier, 1979. Practical implications on RCIA for the parish. Most constructive.

Levinson, Daniel J., editor and author. *The Seasons of a Man's Life.* New York: Ballantine Books, 1978. Presents a fourfold division of the stages of a man's life from behavioral points of view. Useful in spiritual guidance.

Lewinski, Ron. *Guide for Sponsors,* revised edition. Chicago: Liturgy Training Publications, 1980, 1987. Companion to *Finding and Forming Sponsors and Godparents.* Lewinski's excellent book has been tried and proven for eight years throughout the U.S.

_______________. *Welcoming the New Catholic*. Chicago: Liturgy Training Publications, 1983. Discusses the stages of the RCIA and the ministries needed.

Lopresti, James J. "Community Mystagogy." *Catechumenate: A Journal of Christian Initiation* 10 (May 1988): 2–10. Superb treatment of mystagogy as community building and peacemaking.

Made, Not Born: New Perspectives on Christians and the Catechumenate. Liturgical Studies: The Murphy Center for Liturgical Research. Notre Dame: University of Notre Dame Press, 1976.

McBrien, Richard P. *Catholicism*. Minneapolis: Winston Press, 1981. Theological perspectives on the Roman Catholic church.

McKinney, OSB, Mary Benet. *Sharing Wisdom: A Process for Group Decision Making*. Valencia CA: Tabor Publishing, 1987. Mature and spiritually literate discussion of building a community according to the call of Vatican II. Practical steps, problems, models are all tested.

Nelson, Gertrud Mueller. *To Dance with God: Family Ritual and Community Celebration*. New York: Paulist Press, 1986. How to build the bridge between liturgy and the home for the whole church year: fasting, feasting, remembering, imagining, praying. Superb, refreshing.

Nouwen, Henri J. M. *A Cry for Mercy: Prayers from the Genesee*. Garden City: Doubleday, 1983. A short and encouraging book of prayers, suggestions and recommendations for prayer and examples of various prayer forms.

_______________. *Reaching Out: The Three Movements of the Spiritual Life*. Garden City: Doubleday, 1975. Movement to inner self, to fellow human beings, to God. Excellent.

Osborne, Kenan B. *The Christian Sacraments of Initiation: Baptism, Confirmation, Eucharist*. New York: Paulist Press, 1987.

Pawlikowski, John T. "The American Catholic Church As a Public Church." *New Theology Review* 1 (February 1988): 3–37.

Philbert, Paul J. "Catholic Faith Inventory: A Tool for the Catechumenate." *The Living Light* 23, no. 1: 22–29. The author reports on the Catholic Faith Inventory, a resource designed to help catechumens clarify Christian attitudes and doctrinal understanding and to provide pastoral leaders with a guide.

Powell, Karen Hinman. *How to Form a Catechumenate Team.* Chicago: Liturgy Training Publications, 1986. Contains good examples of reflection questions and sample sessions.

Powell, Karen Hinman and Joseph Sinwell, editors. *Breaking Open the Word of God: Cycles A, B, C.* New York: Paulist Press, 1986, 1987, 1988. Some find this resource helpful for Sunday dismissal sessions.

Rahner, Karl. *The Practice of Faith: A Handbook of Contemporary Spirituality.* New York: Crossroad, 1983. Solid, complete, insightful guide to the practice of faith by the leading Catholic theologian of the 20th century.

Rite of Christian Initiation of Adults: Ritual Edition. Chicago: Liturgy Training Publications, 1988. For presider's use at altar. Elegant and easy to read.

Rite of Christian Initiation of Adults: Study Edition. Chicago: Liturgy Training Publications, 1988. For planning and preparing. Necessary for sponsor coordinators and other ministers.

Schmemann, Alexander. *Of Water and the Spirit: A Liturgical Study of Baptism.* New York: St. Vladimir's Seminary Press, 1974. Classic spiritual approach to baptism and confirmation. The mystery of water, procession into the kingdom, the churching.

Searle, Mark, editor. *Baptism and Confirmation.* Alternative Futures for Worship 2. Collegeville: The Liturgical Press, 1988. Includes excellent articles by Searle, Andrew Thompson, Herbert Anderson, Gail Ramshaw, Robert Duggan and Stephen Happel on infant baptism, baptism in stages, RCIA, the experience of parishes. The most competent of this Collegeville series.

______________. "Issues in Christian Initiation: Uses and Abuses of the RCIA." *The Living Light* 22, no. 3. The reunification of the sacraments of initiation has restored powerfully in a single liturgy what it means to be Christian.

______________. *Liturgy Made Simple.* Collegeville: The Liturgical Press, 1981. An insightful, easy and beautiful walk through the meaning of the liturgical life of Catholics.

Simcoe, Mary Ann, editor. *The Liturgy Documents.* Chicago: Liturgy Training Publications, 1985. A must-have parish resource on liturgy. Official statements from the Vatican Council and the National Council of Catholic Bishops on the liturgical calendar, children, music and environment and art.

Twelve Steps and Twelve Traditions. New York: Alcoholics Anonymous World Services, Inc., 1952. Catechumenate sponsors function like A.A. sponsors. This book shows how.

Wallis, Jim. *The Call to Conversion*. San Francisco: Harper and Row, 1981. Practical and insightful presentation on spirituality and peace and justice.

______________. *The Rise of Christian Conscience: The Emergence of a Dramatic Renewal Movement in Today's Church*. Interdenominational discussion of the roots of conscience, nonviolence, civil disobedience and hope.

Walsh, Michael and Brian Davies, editors. *Proclaiming Justice and Peace: Documents from John XXIII to John Paul II*. Mystic CT: Twenty-Third Publications, 1984. Though not up-to-date, excellent collection of encyclicals concerning peace and justice.

Whitehead, James D. and Evelyn Eaton Whitehead. *The Emerging Laity: Returning Leadership to the Community of Faith*. Garden City: Doubleday, 1986.

Yarnold, Edward. *The Awe Inspiring Rites of Initiation: Baptismal Homilies of the Fourth Century*. Slough, England: St. Paul Publications, 1971. Especially helpful for mystagogical reflection.

Young, James J. *Divorcing, Believing, Belonging*. New York: Paulist Press, 1984. Balanced and sensitive approach by a Catholic priest.

Contributors

SANDRA A. CHAKERES is director of religious education at St. Paul's Church, Englewood, Ohio.

JOHN M. HUELS, a priest of the Servite order, is assistant professor of canon law at Catholic Theological Union, Chicago.

MARY EVELYN JEGEN, SND, was the first executive director of Bread for the World Educational Fund and is current vice president of Pax Christi International. She is an adjunct professor at Creighton University, Omaha, and at Trinity College, Washington DC. Her books include *How You Can Be a Peacemaker, Following the Nonviolent Jesus* and *Spark of Light—Center of Love: A Study of the Encyclical, Pacem in Terris.*

ARTURO J. PEREZ of the archdiocese of Chicago is pastor of St. Casimir Parish, Chicago.

EDWARD SELLNER is associate professor of Pastoral Theology and Spirituality at the College of St. Catherine, St. Paul, Minnesota. A former chemical dependency counselor, he has had numerous articles published in the United States, Ireland, England and Germany on lay ministry and spirituality. He is chair of the National Association for Lay Ministry (NALM).

JULIA UPTON, RSM, is associate professor in the theology department at St. John's University, New York, and author of *Journey into Ministry: Companion to the* RCIA.

JAMES A. WILDE is editor of *Catechumenate: A Journal of Christian Initiation* and general editor of the Font and Table Series for Liturgy Training Publications, Chicago.